Mull and the Clearances

Mull and the Clearances

Peter Angus Macnab

ORIGIN

First published in 2024 by Origin
an imprint of Birlinn Ltd
West Newington House
10 Newington Road
Edinburgh
EH9 1QS
www.birlinn.co.uk

ISBN: 978 1 83983 060 0

British Library Cataloguing in Publication Data
A catalogue record for this book is available from the British Library

FSC
www.fsc.org
MIX
Paper | Supporting responsible forestry
FSC® C011748

Printed and bound in Great Britain by
Ashford Colour Ltd, Gosport

Contents

Peter Macnab's original text was written in 2002 but has remained unpublished until now. The Publisher is grateful to Mull author Jean Whittaker for her editorial work in preparing the book for publication. As well as her introduction she has added some notes through Peter's text with updates on what has happened since it was written.

Foreword

by

Sally Magnusson

I have always loved knowing that my family hails in part from the ravishing isle of Mull. But my appreciation of this Hebridean heritage has a darker side. My people didn't leave Mull because they wanted to, but because – like so many others described by Peter Macnab in these pages – they were forced to. And the life they lived afterwards was a hard one.

From early on in my own life, growing up in a comfortable home in the town of Rutherglen on the outskirts of Glasgow, I was encouraged to remember that only a generation separated us from poverty and privation. My mother, Mamie Baird, spent her own Rutherglen childhood in the straitened circumstances common to working class folk in the 1930s. Among her fund of anecdotes was a figure who cropped up again and again. This was her granny, her father's mother, Annie Baird (née McEachern) from Mull – one of the stream of migrant Highlanders who went south after the Clearances.

Annie died when Mamie was still quite young, but she remembered her all her life. My mother talked about the feisty pride that had Annie sailing along the Rutherglen streets so grandly that she was nicknamed the Duchess, though she took in washing for a living and timed her arrival at the butcher's shop for the exact moment when prices would be reduced at the end of the day. My mother remembered the tickle of Annie's horsehair sofa under her bare legs, the soft Hebridean accent, the Gaelic songs she used to sing to herself in the evenings with tears streaming down her cheeks.

My mother also told me a wonderful story about the family cow.

When Annie was born in Mull in 1850, during the cataclysmic period of clearance which Peter narrates here, her father James was a tenant farmer in the township of Ardmore, a settlement by the sea a few miles north of Tobermory. There he eked a chancy livelihood from cattle and shared crops. As the story was passed down to me, the family struggled on after James died with little to their name except one cow for milk and butter. The cow was every family's lifeline. That also made it the possession most vulnerable to a landowner looking for ways to force inhabitants off the land to make way for more profitable sheep.

'The day came when it was our family's turn to lose their cow,' my mother said. 'It was taken from them, along with other cows from neighbouring crofts, and put on an islet off Tobermory known as Calve Island. And to their amazement, that cow came back. Somehow it had managed to swim right across the Sound of Mull again and walk back to the family croft. It was thought to be a tremendous thing, that a cow should help the family resist eviction by swimming home.'

Researching the story, I discovered my folks living in a sizeable community in Ardmore in the 1850s, full of different crafts. At some point, perhaps around 1855, James died and his unmarried older brother Allan McEachern became responsible for his sister-in-law Christina and her three daughters, including little Annie. Difficult times followed: cattle prices had plummeted and Allan was already elderly. Poring through the records, I turned up the outcome of an application for poor relief in February 1858: 'Allan McEachern Ardmore refused on the ground that he is able-bodied and has a cow.'

It was so moving to see those words. Here was my family living in obvious penury, but they did have a cow. And maybe the return of that cow, after it was taken, helped them to hold out against the 'flit and remove' eviction notices which the Ardmore community, like every other, ignored for as long as possible, because most of these folk had absolutely nowhere to go. But leave they all had to in the end. The McEacherns were among the last of the Ardmore inhabitants to be evicted in 1863.

Bleakly I scanned the next census return for Ardmore. There was only one resident left: a shepherd.

My folk joined the roll call, by then in the tens of thousands, of people displaced in the Clearances. We know that some of those people – notably those with health and vigour and the means to afford a passage abroad – managed to forge interesting, prosperous lives as immigrants on the other side of the world, and their descendants today are rightly proud of that endeavour. But for a probable majority of cleared people, emigrating was never an option. Many, many former inhabitants of townships like Ardmore ended their days in penury or drifted to cities like Glasgow, where they crammed into overcrowded tenements of unimaginable squalor and rampant disease. That was my people's story.

When they left Ardmore, Annie's mother Christina and uncle Allan, by then both registered paupers, moved with the children into one of the slums at the top of Tobermory's Back Brae, an area already teeming with the destitute from other cleared townships across the island. There the adults were put to outside labour, while young Annie and her sisters joined the queue for the daily steamer to the Clydeside ports in search of work. At the age of thirteen, my great-grandmother went into domestic service in Glasgow. Later, to escape the fetid air of the city that contributed to the deaths from TB of her husband and three of their four children, she moved across the Clyde to Rutherglen. Her surviving child became my grandfather, John Baird. As I say, a hard life.

In summarising what lay behind the Clearances Peter Macnab is fair and judicious, although occasionally his indignation bursts through at what he describes as an 'obnoxious class system, a form of Apartheid, if you like, where the Common Herd, especially the peasantry, were treated as near aborigines.'

And he's not wrong there. The clearances of Glencalvie and Greenyards in the Ross-shire valley of Strathcarron were happening around the same time as those on Mull reached their zenith. When I was researching that period for my novel Music in the Dark, I was shocked to discover that the government in London regarded the mass emigration of Gaels from the Highlands as an opportunity to replace them with 'racially superior people of Teutonic stock'. Sir Charles Trevelyan at the Treasury believed that the Germans ('an orderly, moral, industrious and frugal people, less foreign to us than the Irish or Scotch Celt') would assimilate nicely. The proposal was tantamount to ethnic cleansing.

This is the world that Peter Macnab presents to us here, first by exploring the wider context and then by itemising the Mull evictions estate by estate. He names the landowners; he names some of the people whose livelihoods, culture and very lives were held in such little regard.

In my own family's sweet place across the sound from Ardnamurchan, where salt is carried on the wind and a cow once made her way home, nothing is left among the tumbled stone of past dwellings, except bracken.

And here am I, more than a century and a half after my great-grandmother boarded the steamer for Glasgow, still cheering on a cow – and still aching for the many who, during one of the most shameful periods in the history of Britain, were literally of less value than beasts.

Introduction
by
Jean Whittaker

Peter Macnab's association with and love of Mull was lifelong – and a very long life at that. Born in 1903, he came to Mull as a little boy of three, when his father was appointed as the governor of the Mull Combination Poorhouse, and he died in 2002 at the age of 98.

My first meeting with Peter Macnab must have been in 1979. In that year Peter and his family, having holidayed in Mull over many years, finally managed to have a house built in Dervaig, and from then on he was a more frequent visitor to Mull, usually in the trout season. I can see him yet, leaning over the partitioned trays in which trout and salmon flies were displayed for sale in Tackle & Books. At that time, I was fairly new to the island and my bible was Macnab's *The Isle of Mull*, in the prestigious Islands series published by David and Charles, but any awe that I might have felt in first meeting its author was quickly dispelled by a shared passion for fishing and by Peter's geniality. I can hear him as well now as I can see him, examining a nicely tied white moth and recommending it for sea trout – cast gently towards the dam wall at the end of Loch Torr just as dusk stole over the loch.

This passion for angling had its origins in his early life in Achafraoch House, the name that was given to the Poorhouse at Newdale, where the family lived in the governor's flat on the top floor and where the Tobermory River flowed past a few yards from the wall at the Poorhouse's northern end. It was in this river that Peter made his first adventures into angling – from the impetuous rush to seize a fork and get worms out of the Poorhouse midden and the careful stalking and patient waiting by the pools of the little Tobermory River, to the time when he graduated to a fly rod and became an expert with it. For a young boy, the countryside ramblings around the isolated building at Newdale, provided adventures and made him something of a naturalist. With the optimism of youth, and with what may have been a paternalistic colonial outlook taken from his father, who had retired from the Hong Kong police, he saw the Poorhouse as an institution built by the parish councils for the good of their people to care for the needy and the elderly. Some of these, if not victims of the Clearances themselves, were probably the sons and daughters of those who had been evicted or were emigrants during mid-century decades of the Clearances. With his father as resident governor, and with a visiting doctor, Baptist minister and Inspector of Poor, any underlying tensions at the institution were not the business of a growing boy.

If fishing was his first love, golf was his other leisure enthusiasm whilst still a schoolboy. The third of Tobermory's golf courses opened in 1907 close to his home at Newdale, and Peter's first interest was limited to the finding of lost golf balls in order to obtain the elastic inside as a propellant for catapults. By the 1920s, there was a little corrugated-iron clubhouse with a veranda, and Peter was a player and competitor among the 50 persons on its membership list. Aged 17, he went as a junior to work in the Clydesdale Bank in Tobermory, and before long he started to move up the promotional ladder at the Bank with an appointment in Glasgow, then Rothesay and finally West Kilbride, where he married and where his retirement marked the end of 41 years' service to the Bank. After 1979, when his house in Dervaig was built, he and his wife became regular visitors. By this time, the Poorhouse had long been closed and stood as a gaunt ruin until 1970, before it was demolished and the stone taken away to Tobermory and used to extend a stubby pier at Ledaig, the Sinclair Pier, to which the Distillery laid claim. For 20 years this remained as a crude rubble pier occasionally used as a helicopter landing pad. Eventually it, in its turn, was incorporated into the car park and all that remains of the Poorhouse now lies under roadway, parking spaces and the rip-rap sea wall.

Peter would not have regretted its passing, being a man who always looked forward. Nevertheless, his early life in the Poorhouse left him with a strong social and moral conscience that led him to write about the Clearances. His later banking career made him a good listener and he had become the sort of person who was at ease with almost anyone, and they with him. Always an affable man, he took pleasure in hearing stories and putting on paper accounts of the surroundings, the folklore and the eccentric and entertaining characters which made up the scenes of life in Mull in the last decades of the twentieth century. After his retirement, he became a regular contributor to the *Scots Magazine*, with more than a couple of dozen articles on Mull on topics ranging from geological oddities through fok-lore and archaeology to funeral customs, all showing his deep curiosity and interest in the island in which he was proud to call himself a teuchter – a country man. From the cutting of the peats to the netting of an illicit salmon, he knew the ways and wiles of the country folk. Even then, his benevolence and humour extended to the estate factor who had been outwitted by the teuchter, when the teuchter departed along with the salmon or sea trout that had been taken from under the noses of the laird's watchers.

It is this sense of social justice that informs his account of the Clearances. Many of the crofters of the time were strangely unwilling to criticise the new landowners, still seeing in them the old chiefs of the past, whose responsibility was to look after the clan – their children. Most of the crofters' anger was directed at the factors, agents of the chief, such as the dreaded Factor Mor, Chamberlain to the Duke of Argyll, who was responsible for clearances and emigration in the south and Ross of Mull.

In the pages that follow, Peter Macnab takes us through the Mull Estates, landowner by landowner, apportioning responsibility squarely upon the landowners without condoning the methods by which the factors and their henchmen executed their orders from above. To some extent, he tempers his judgments from harsh to more reasonable, giving occasional mention of schemes that were designed to alleviate the dire economic situation in which all found themselves.

The reserving of what had been common land for private use he abhors and in his own day, the opening up of land and water for islanders and the public was something that he wanted for all. In 1990, when in his 80s, he recalled to memory the joy that the stream running past the Poorhouse had given him, and approached the local fishing-tackle shops to get their support for a scheme to make this small river a salmon and seatrout water. This scheme he proposed to submit to the Forestry Commission. All that would be needed was some blasting work on the cascades of the Eas Brae, some means of bypassing the hydroelectric dam and, perhaps, some way of negotiating the waterfall above the pool below Baliscate ('The Black Pool') should this be necessary. Surely, he wrote persuasively, 'a grant would be available on the Tourist/Environmental basis for this work. In this way, angling facilities would be brought into being that would be conveniently accessible and generate a profit in which the Forestry Commission would share handsomely.' It is so typical of Peter Macnab that, almost to the end of his life, when he was writing this book, he was still full of enthusiasm about new things to communicate to another generation.

Part 1

The Clearances in the Highlands and Islands

1
The Background of the Clearances

Before I write about the Clearances in Mull, I think it would be helpful to understand the background of the Clearances in the Highlands and Islands, as there are sometimes misapprehensions about the whole subject. Why, one person writing in the press recently argued that they did not happen!

When the Jacobite uprisings and Culloden were over and the military policing easier, social conditions settled down temporarily, and population, which had been expanding to a point where one-fifth of the population of Scotland was living in one-third or the land – the Highlands. In modern times these figures are nearer two-thirds in one-tenth – the Lowlands. In the Highlands the land now had to support larger families, and be divided into still smaller units, which resulted in living conditions approaching subsistence levels at times, worsened by the occasional bad season and poor crop returns. The increasing popularity of the potato greatly helped an otherwise monotonous diet; by the mid-nineteenth century it formed 80% of the family fare. Population was exceeding resources. Depopulation had to come; the evil lies in the manner in which this was forcibly achieved, especially during the twenty peak years between 1840 and 1860. Local evictions had happened from the 1770s onwards through the actions of a few unscrupulous landowners.

One of the few sympathetic lairds was James Matheson, of the famous Hong Kong firm of Jardine Matheson, a man of great wealth arising from the opium trade in the Far East. When he retired to his native Scotland, he bought the island of Lewis. During the dark days of the mid-nineteenth century he spent a fortune of over £250,000 in providing food for the hard-pressed crofters, as well as financial support through work such as road-building, fencing, drainage, harbours and jetties. Further, he gave the use of his own yacht free of charge to seasonal workers from the Hebrides at harvest time in the south. Certainly he did have a few evictions in his estates, but they are attributed to the actions of an over-enthusiastic factor, and alternative holdings were provided in Barra. He also gave full financial support to people wishing to emigrate.

There were four critical periods:

1. About 1800, when the old communal system of run-rig agriculture merged into individual crofting. The introduction of sheep was now beginning to be felt.

2. The catastrophe of the potato disease in 1846/7, which led to the harsh and well-documented evictions, poverty and emigration.

3. Migration and emigration.

4. The Napier Commission of 1883 and onwards, the outcome of press and private pressures that forced the government into taking belated action.

2
Crofting

Under the old run-rig system, strips of land were cultivated on a system of rotation, changing every three years to prevent the continual use of the best land by one person. The real source of cash income was black cattle, the Highland Kyloe, much in demand for its quality in the south. They depended entirely on communal hill grazings, where the numbers of livestock were carefully managed by the community in order to provide fair grazings for all. This was based on the equation – 'One horse = four cattle or stirks = thirty sheep'. That is where that peculiar expression originated: 'Grazing entitlement is one leg of a horse', i.e. one quarter of the relevant equation figure.

There were three classes of tenants loosely defined by the rents they paid. There was first of all the tacksman, who paid a rent or 'Tack' to the landowner in excess of £50 per year. (The figures are approximate.) He was something of a privileged person, perhaps a friend or relative of the laird, who was allowed to sub-let surplus land to crofters and cottars and retain the rents, also to demand their services when required. Next were the crofters, paying rents not exceeding £20 per annum. They were granted legal rights of tenure for a fixed period, with renewal subject to the consent of the landowner.

Finally, the cottars, who were greatly in the majority, in fact they formed 95% of the total tenancy and paid 74% of the total rents. Their rents varied from £10 downwards. They had no legal rights of tenure at all, occupying their holdings by use and wont as their forefathers had done during the days of the Clan System, which has been described as 'The most benevolent form of Feudalism in Europe.' Under the Clan System, now gone for ever, the lands were not the property of the chiefs, but of the whole clan, of which he was father-figure for the whole conduct of the clan, which in turn supported him in every way. Both crofters and cottars are often loosely referred to as 'crofters' for simplicity in the later text.

The cot-houses of the time were primitive and insanitary, according to our standards, and child mortality was high. They are called 'black houses', but it is held by some that this somewhat derogatory term should be 'thatched houses' through the close similarity of the pronunciation of the two Gaelic words for black and thatched: Tigh Dubh and Tigh Tugath. They were stoutly built with double drystone walls, the space between filled with dried peat to exclude draughts. A peat fire burned in the centre of the room, giving off smoke and soot which escaped through an opening in the roof. That is why old furnishings were low-set, to keep below the smoke level. The house was shared by the livestock behind a flimsy partition, with a sloping floor for obvious reasons! It was not until the beginning of the nineteenth century that a proper chimney and fireplace were built into one of the gables of the later houses.

Early visitors who ventured into the Highlands and Islands wrote scathingly about the living conditions of the people, ignoring the clean air and healthy exacting work outside. Such critics could better have turned their attention to the disease-ridden, overcrowded, insanitary slums of the mainland cities, from which originated the epidemics that spread nationwide.

By the end of the eighteenth century a new race of landowners had become established, wealthy men who took over lands confiscated when the chiefs fled abroad or had been deprived of all their powers and influence. They knew and cared nothing about the traditional ways of the people. More reprehensible were many of the new generation of resident clan chiefs now that their old ties with the clan were gone. They simply became lairds and owners of the lands of their clansfolk.

The cottars became easy prey to be sacrificed for the introduction of sheep and the new 'Improvements.' It is true that the old system of crofting was uneconomic. Large open areas formed by the amalgamation of crofts were easier to run, more productive, and yielded higher rents. An unwanted population had to go.

Although crofting conditions became uncertain after 1770, they remained at least tolerable into the early nineteenth century, although always subjected to increasing rents. The menace of sheep was steadily getting worse. It was found that the Highlands and Islands provided excellent grazings for the Cheviot and hardy black-faced sheep, which were larger and heavier than the small indigenous sheep that had been kept mostly for its wool.

Sheep were so much more profitable than cattle, so landowners turned to this new source of income. A typical sheep farm carried at least 2,000 sheep. However, the sheep boom ended in the early 1870s, when mutton and wool began to flood into the country from developing Australia and New Zealand. By this time, too, the grazing habits of sheep had ruined the grazings, souring the land, which was now avoided by cattle. Sheep runs reverted to heather, bracken and scrub, and towards the end of the century were useless for anything other than increasingly fashionable sporting estates.

Slow at first to cash in on the profitable sheep, landlords hardened their hearts and began to take every chance to dispossess the peasantry, perhaps moving them to new holdings where the land was poor and difficult to cultivate – but with no reduction in rents. The first direct evictions took place in the lands of Macdonnell of Glengarry in 1785, when 500 tenants were summarily removed, leaving their homeland by the emigrant ship Macdonald at Fort William. Local evictions started in Ross-shire and elsewhere in the 1790s, but the final clearance of the people began in the 1820s.

During the Napoleonic Wars the kelp industry provided some relief for coastal communities. It began when the calcined ash of the kelp was found to be an effective substitute for the barilla that could no longer be imported from the Continent. Kelp, or soda ash, used in the glass and linen industries ('alginates' in modern times) was produced by drying and burning seaware, the best being the Laminaria, the familiar 'Tangle o' the Isles', which is half exposed in great beds along rocky shores at low tide and washed ashore in late autumn. Gathering kelp was a hard life for the crofters, who could earn around £5 for a year's work by a whole family. The landowners collected as much as £20 per ton during the height of the operations – £10-15,000 per year in the best locations. It is recorded that the incidence of arthritis and rheumatic disorders were never worse than during this period, brought on by the constant soakings and exposure.

I was told by some old men in Mull that to drink an infusion of the leaves of the bog bean that floats on most of the pools in the boglands gave some relief. Crofters were often forbidden to use seaweed as the usual fertiliser for cultivation, so greedy were landlords for maximum profits. The industry came to an end when imports from Europe were restored after the wars. Many landowners had begun to cash in on this new source of income, and helped by improving communications were enjoying a new but expensive social life. This still further intensified the impositions on their tenants to replace the lost income.

Mull produced about 600 tons of kelp ash annually, 8.5% of the total production of the western seaboard.

3
The Potato Disease and Its Aftermath

Uneasy crofting conditions came to a tragic end in the mid-1840s, when the people were faced with a fresh calamity – the potato disease, which at one stroke destroyed the one crop on which the people depended for survival. This disease, Phytophthora infestans, was a wind-blown fungus that first appeared in America in 1843. It spread to Europe, where it first appeared in Belgium, and from there it reached Ireland in 1845, where its virulence and rapidity quickly brought the population to near starvation. In fact, the government had to provide immediate relief by bringing maize flour from North America. Bad though conditions became soon after in Scotland, they were not to be compared with the tragedy of Ireland, where about two million people died or emigrated between 1845 and 1851, for they had become almost totally dependent on potatoes as a main diet

In 1846 and 1847 the full fury of the disease fell on the mild humid areas of the Highlands. A whole crop could be reduced to an uneatable pulp in one day. The clergy submitted that the blight was an act of God, a punishment for the sins of the people, and should not be interfered with by giving relief. The government allowed itself to be persuaded by this nonsense, although as a sop to its hypocrisy it suggested that it was a matter for the landowners. At that time the clergy were appointed by or with the approval of the landowners, so with this Victorian economic rectitude the government at first ignored its duty to the hard-pressed peasantry. This was left to local Parish Councils and the Kirk Sessions of the churches. No wonder that in 1843 what is known as the Disruption of the Churches took place, where a large number of ministers broke away from the State church and set up the Free Church.

The distant government was in any case tied up with foreign wars, acquisition of colonies, Irish politics and putting down slavery abroad with the help of that same navy that was helping to force the use of opium on the Chinese – far too busy to concern itself with the exploitation of women and children in industry, or the heartless extinction of a race of people at home. The parliament was composed of wealthy landowners, the aristocracy, and industrialists, who naturally acted in their own interests.

Although superstitious, the people were highly religious, and resigned to this Divine punishment. If you are ever at Bonar Bridge, turn west into 12-mile Strath Carron until you come to a dead end at Croick church, centre of the infamous Glen Calvie evictions. Here, scratched on one of the diamond window panes (now preserved under glass), you will read such short messages as 'Glen Calvie people the wicked generation' with the date, inscribed during the days when the only refuge the people could find was in the churchyard. Any idea of sheltering inside Croick church would have been considered desecration. The three Statistical Accounts published from the 1790s onwards, describing the conditions in Highland parishes, were compiled nearly always by ministers or landowners, with no mention of the evictions or the hardships of the people. It was not until 1883 that the public was made aware of the past 100 years of oppression and hardship.

Faced now with starvation, and with rents always on the increase, the people were bewildered and leaderless, for so many of the tacksmen and crofters who could afford to do so had left the country. Fishing did help coastal communities, and such game as could be picked up without incurring the wrath of the landowners. A central Relief Board was set up, and quantities of oatmeal, barley and peas began to arrive by ship. Tobermory was one of the distributional centres. The government still considered Relief to be the responsibility of the landowners, but at last began to give grudging support.

Relief rations were distributed in exchange for hard work on public services such as road-making, bridges, drainage and wall building. In the 100 years that followed the passing of the eighteenth-century Enclosures Act, no less than an estimated 10,000 miles of dry-stone walls were built in Scotland. To this day the term 'Destitution Road' is applied to some of the roads built during the period, such as the lonely stretch across the moorlands between Braemore and Dundonnel. Walking distance for the workers were sometimes unbelievable, but were not taken into consideration for working time. The old and infirm sometimes had to struggle as best they could to the centres of distribution.

In Mull, the first road on which a carriage could be driven was built by this labour between Auchnacraig (at Grass Point, nearest ferry-point to Oban) and the village of Salen. However, work was not confined to public utilities. The lairds were the ones appointed to administer the distribution of food. Some of them directed the labour to carrying out improvements on their own private estates, the work paid for by food from the public supplies. There were even reports later by a few witnesses that lairds had been quietly feeding their livestock with grain from the same source.

More and more people had to leave their holdings to face a life of destitution and pauperism. This was the period when local authorities, driven by the financial burden of Relief, decided it would be cheaper and more effective to erect several poorhouses, such as the Mull Combination Poorhouse at Tobermory, about which I have written elsewhere in detail. Institutions that would care for the homeless were financed by a consortium of parishes, such as in the case of the Tobermory Poorhouse, built in 1862 and financed by three Mull parishes plus those of Moidart, Morven, Ardnamurchan and the islands of Coll and Tiree.

Excellent and well thought-out as this scheme proved to be, it was after all a temporary expedient whose usefulness ended with the nineteenth century, when living conditions were stabilised and independence gained for the old folk when the Old Age Pensioners' Act was passed in 1909, awarding a pension of 5 shillings (22½p) per week. With hindsight, it was thought that a better idea would have been to have those unfortunate people cared for in their own communities. The best was done in the exacting circumstances of the times.

The impact of the potato disease was a long-awaited excuse for some of the more impatient landowners to carry out immediate evictions of this unwanted peasantry. One excellent solution was by emigration – compulsory and otherwise – which the landlords hastened to exploit.

4
Migration and Emigration

From the earliest times, when crofting became increasingly precarious, there was always a slow drift to the industrial south, where prospects were better. The older people who were traditionally peasant farmers were slow to adapt to the new jobs in the growing heavy industries. Every year at harvest time there was a seasonal return journey made to the farmlands of the south, especially by the younger people. The few pounds they brought home greatly helped the family budget. Cash was always scarce in the Highlands and Islands, and barter a regular medium of exchange. Up to about 1815 there was a national scarcity of coin in Scotland. At the time of the Treaty of Union in 1707 the coinage was so scarce and debased that one of the clauses of the Act promised an immediate review, and a restoration of quantity and quality. This was not implemented until 100 years later. The Scottish Mint in Edinburgh was closed and its functions transferred to the south.

The seasonal migration of harvesters reminds me that up to twenty or so years ago, before mechanical digging took over, I used to see gangs of potato-lifters who came over from Ireland to work in our extensive potato fields. They lived in bothies or farm outhouses, which would have been the same conditions as experienced by our migrant Highlanders. In 1822 there was the tragic loss of the smack Mary of Iona conveying forty-four harvesters from Iona and the Ross of Mull that cast a gloom for years over the whole community. She sank after a collision with a tug in the Clyde; only two men and two women were saved.

Emigration was a different story. It was started on a small scale by tacksmen in the 1770s when landlords were beginning to find that the conditions of the 'tack' were over-generous, such as the rights to retain rents from sub-letting. By raising the rents and curtailing entitlements, it was sought to get rid of this class of tenant. Anticipating trouble ahead, and when financially able to do so, they began to leave the country for destinations abroad where there were genuine prospects of an assured future. They left in ships of their own choice and in such comfort as those ships provided. They were followed by wise crofters who could afford to do so, when the going was still good, so to speak Those early emigrants usually became well established in the developing colonies, where their energy and initiative found scope, and their favourable reports encouraged the people at home to follow their example. Sufficient starting capital was the answer, and the many thousands who lacked this were disappointed as the years went on. North America was the favoured destination, with settlements developing, especially around the Great Lakes. There is a 'Tobermory', now a large town on a peninsula on the south side of Lake Huron. Australia and New Zealand came next in popularity. Among many Scottish placenames there is another 'Tobermory', a settlement in central Queensland of all places! By the end of the nineteenth century there were few corners of the world where Scots folk were not to be found. I've even read that Gaelic is still spoken by the descendants of some emigrants in Patagonia!

In Hong Kong, perhaps the greatest company in the Far East, Jardine Matheson & Company, was founded by William Jardine, who came from Dumfries, and James Matheson, from Lairg – I've mentioned his good works in Lewis earlier. Wherever possible, they made it a point to engage clerks from Scotland. They had both started as clerks in Calcutta before settling in Hong Kong early in the nineteenth century. Matheson retired to Lewis with a huge fortune from the opium trade, and spent vast sums improving the island and financing emigration.

At home crofters were now defenceless against the actions of impatient lairds. Massive evictions followed the potato catastrophe, and their holdings were turned into sheep farms – or large agricultural units. Finding emigration a convenient way of clearing the land, some landlords were even prepared to subsidise the fares of emigrants. Some of the victims, torn between nostalgia for the old settled days of their forefathers, threatened with pauperism and a futureless life at home, considered that even the unknown conditions overseas could be no worse, perhaps much better, if they were to believe some of the reports sent home by earlier emigrants. They paid their own fares if they could scrape the cash together, selling their livestock and anything that could be turned into money, leaving them penniless in an inhospitable environment. Fares ranged widely from £3.50 for an individual to £35 for a large family.

Unscrupulous shipowners attracted many with their glowing descriptions of the comfort of the voyage, with lands just awaiting their arrival for the start of a happy new life. The fine new land turned out to be a bleak shore, the land a forest which had to be cleared before cultivation could begin. Emigrants often faced greater hardships than at home, depending on gifts from earlier settlers to tide them over a winter of starvation. Too many emigrant ships were overcrowded, barely seaworthy, food and water scarce and the water barely drinkable. Some ships were even ex-slavers. Disease often broke out in the insanitary 'tween-decks – cholera, typhus, smallpox; in fact in 1847, between the shore quarantines that had to be set up and on shipboard, deaths ran into thousands. It was no uncommon voyage that found 10% of the passengers had died. It is true that those were the very worst conditions, but they were a shocking fact. There were also the well-founded ships which were sometimes inspected by shore officials – too seldom the case – where the emigrants were reasonably looked after. One such ship was the *Brilliant*, that left Tobermory for Australia in 1837. Tobermory was a centre for the departure of emigrants from other parts of Mull, from Calgary to Bunessan.

This sad state of affairs peaked between 1840 and 1860, by which time conditions had at least stabilised for the reduced number of tenants who could afford to pay the exorbitant rents. The potato disease returned, but temporarily and on a small scale. Evictions and emigration continued on a reducing scale compared with what had gone before. By the end of the nineteenth century, 20,000 people had emigrated from the Highlands and Islands. The figure for the overall reduction in population would have been much greater, but those were the years of large families, where the number of births exceeded that of deaths.

5

The Napier Commission of 1883

I have referred to the absence of leadership and the acceptance of their fate by the victims of the Clearances. It was not until 1882 that exasperated crofters began to rebel. The most serious trouble began in Skye with what became known as the 'Battle of the Braes'. Here, in Lord MacDonald's parish of Braes, a number of tenants boldly moved their cattle back to former, but now forbidden pastures. He retorted by issuing legal notices of evictions against the culprits, with a demand for the immediate payment of all rents. The officer whose duty it was to hand over those notices was waylaid and the documents burned. A body of police was called in, but opposed by the protestors, and not being happy about this particular duty, they retired. Even when the military were called in there was stubborn resistance.

Crofters everywhere began to join the Highland League, with protest meetings being held all over the country: but the most effective support came from outside. Alexander MacKenzie, who had been agitating for years with little response, attended a meeting in Inverness, where he commented forcibly that while the government was setting up a committee to discuss the scarcity of crabs and lobsters, was it not more urgent to take up the wretched plight of the people of the Highlands and Islands? The local Member of Parliament – I do not have his name – who had attended the meeting was so impressed and sympathetic that he raised the matter forcibly in the House of Commons with impressive results. By this time, too, the government had been pressurised by the Press and public opinion; so in 1883 it appointed the Napier Commission to review the whole question, with powers. It arranged hearing with witnesses from all the affected parishes. The outcome appears in the official Books of Court, where in thirty volumes 46,750 questions and answers were recorded. There would have been even more witnesses, but even in the 1880s and '90s there were still intimidation and victimisation by landlords, which discouraged people from coming forward; and indeed there were districts so depopulated that no competent person was left to appear.

To begin with, although it did good work, the Commission was rather less efficient than it might have been, for some of its members were the very lairds who were interested parties. However, the discontented and impatient peasantry in some districts continued to take action that still involved the police and military, which led to the setting up of a better-balanced Commission. Crofters' Acts were to follow, with amendments over the years, that still operate today. Crofters were now given the right to remain in their holdings as long as they paid their rents. The first act of the Commission was an immediate reduction of rents by 40% and the cancellation of unfair arrears. After 100 years security had come, but all too late: the end of an old song and the near-extinction of a race. Yet these pathetic ruins we see, that had been built stone by stone by a vanished people, remain monuments to a shameful period in Scottish history dominated by the privileged, condoned by a distant government.

6
The Later Years

To be fair, if the old conditions could never return, at least Landlordism did create a new way of life and a new style of economic benefits. Early in the nineteenth century, Sir Walter Scott glamorised the Highlands with his romantic writings. He commented on '. . . inhabitants dispossessed by unrelenting avarice . . . Meantime the Highlands may become a fairy ground for romance and poetry.' This brought a new tourist industry into being which expanded widely with the development of roads, railways and sea communications, until today it is the mainstay of the Highlands and Islands. This was further encouraged by the example of Queen Victoria, when she fell in love with the Highlands and built her be-turreted 'Scottish Baronial' castle on Deeside. Her example was eagerly followed by the wealthy and the aristocracy. A Highland estate became a status symbol, and the twelfth of August, when grouse-shooting begins, an important day in the calendar of fashion. With the improvement of sporting guns the grouse became the most valuable bird in the world.

Incongruous mansions, shooting lodges and pseudo castles mushroomed in unspoilt glens. George Scott-Moncrieff cynically summarised this peaceful invasion, 'Balmorality', as he called it, as the 'Glutinous compound of hypocrisy, false sentiment, industrial ugliness, and clammy pseudo-Calvinism!' One thought occurs to me: it is hard to understand how Queen Victoria appeared to be unaware of the evidences of the harsh Clearances she must have seen before her eyes during her Highland journeys. Did she not write – 'There is a great peculiarity about Highlanders, and they are a fine chivalrous active people.' Her affection for the Highlands was genuine.

In the early days of this invasion the new lairds had no hesitation in evicting tenants to use their lands as sites for their impressive new buildings and the surrounding policies. However, they planted valuable woodlands, seen today as mature timber. Money was injected into small country businesses, and the community provided a paid staff for the 'Big House'. Local tradesmen shared a steady income. Extensive farmlands replaced the old scattered, admittedly uneconomic, holdings with walling and drainage, and the introduction of new and valuable crops and improved livestock.

In time the 'Apartheid' ended and a new generation of lairds came to respect and depend on the useful abilities of stalkers, ghillies, estate workers, farm hands, boatmen, and became respected in turn. When I was a boy in Tobermory at the beginning of the twentieth century, there was still a vague feeling that we should touch our caps or forelocks when a laird passed in his carriage or early motor car on his way to 'Sit on the Bench' in the local courthouse to administer justice to the local anti-social miscreants in the town. I think one or two of them really did think it was their due, so deeply entrenched were the traditions of the past. Today estates can be a financial burden; most resident lairds are gentlemen farmers and expert stock-raisers, with a genuine involvement in the community and economy of the area.

In all fairness, there is another side to the story we are apt to forget. The introduction of potatoes, to which we referred earlier, made this vegetable the staple diet of the people as time went on. Settled conditions following the end of the Clan System and Jacobite uprisings, and improving communications, had resulted in larger families and often a subdivision of land to a point where the economy became precarious in many places.

Real famine came with the failure of the potato crops in the 1840s. All that and a new way of life taken up by many of the lairds of the old school, who were desperate for hard cash to maintain the new standards they had created for themselves in the circles of high society in the south. Also, for the maritime lairds, there was the loss of easy money received during the Napoleonic Wars from the highly lucrative kelp industry; finally the practice of their tenants of paying the comparatively low rents in goods, livestock and services instead of hard cash. This was good enough for the old days, but now unprofitable for the lairds.

Depopulation had to come; the evil lay in the harsh methods in which this was carried out, and the blame must be shared by that far-off Victorian government, which allowed these methods to continue unchecked.

If you have read the foregoing, you will find that in the following chapters Mull's story of the Clearances is simply a microcosm of the whole. I am ending with a description of Crofting as it operates today under the Crofters (Scotland) Act.

7
Crofting Then and Now*

Many of us who live on the urbanised mainland still consider there is something romantic in being a crofter. He is his own boss, making his own decisions, associated with the hackneyed word Mañana. One who is supposed to wish –

> Would that the peats would cut themselves
> The fish jump on the shore,
> That I upon my bed might lie
> Henceforth for ever more.

I have had an appealing letter from a young couple in distant Cornwall, tired, as they said, of the sophisticated rat-race, seeking the peace and easy life of a crofter. I gently disabused them and referred them to the Crofters Commission. I heard no more. So I'd just like to tell you something about crofting.

The most dramatic change in the social and agricultural history of the Highlands and Islands followed the findings of the government-appointed Napier Commission of 1883, which was followed by the Crofters Holding Act in 1886 that with amendments was last ratified in 1993, and which operates today with continuing success as the Crofters (Scotland) Act. Just bear with me and I'll give you two examples from the 100 years of landlord-created

**This chapter was written in 2002, so much of the information in it regarding the current state of crofting reflects the situation at that time.*

apartheid from which the crofters suffered. In 1847 the hated factor John Campbell, of the Argyll Estates in the Isle of Mull, said: 'The cottar tribe, who are the locusts on the land . . . must remain a dead weight on His Grace's estates . . . with few exceptions they comprise indolent, uncivilised pauperism . . . His Grace the Duke of Argyll never speculated money to such advantage as to get rid of them with all possible speed.'

And from the crofter-victims' point of view, giving evidence before a meeting of the Napier Commission in 1883, a man from the Ross of Mull observed: 'The harsh and cruel law of evictions formerly used has given way to the more modern and refined mode of grinding away our subject by diminishing our means [exorbitant rents] which will eventually serve the purpose of bringing us to abject poverty.'

Certainly depopulation had to come with a rising population in an area of fixed production. The evil lay in the manner in which this was brought about.

The first action of the Napier Commission was to reduce all rents by 40%, cancel all unfair arrears and ensure security of tenure. The former cottars, who were in a large majority, were now gone, an easy prey for the new generation of landowners, for their holdings had been on the old Clan System of use and wont. Crofters, too, even with legal rights of tenancy, found their rights eroded by every method from charging excessive rents to non-renewal of expired tenancies.

The present Crofters (Scotland) Act is administered by the Crofters Commission, which was formed in

1955. It is a non-departmental public body, an arm of the central government, formed by the Scottish Executive Rural Affairs Department. The main purpose of the Act, and hence of the Commission, is to support the crofting system, which in turn supports rural communities throughout the Highlands and Islands. It is wisely centred in Inverness, conveniently close to Caithness and the four western crofting counties, and the Orkneys and Shetlands. Its latest report gives a detailed picture of crofting today.

There are 17,700 registered holdings with 3,523 owner occupiers, representing 30,000 family members. In fact, crofting covers 25% of the agricultural area of the Highlands and Islands. Broadly, I suggest that the two subjects of security and diversification are the most important.

Today the tenure of a croft is a heritable item in a crofter's moveable estate. It can be very easily transferred to a member of his family, but if to a non-member this must have the permission of the Crofters Commission, a condition which also applies to sub-letting. The Commission must also approve the de-crofting of a holding for use – say – in industry. The crofter is supposed to live no further distant than ten miles from his holding. Last year 83 crofts with absentee tenants were re-allocated to new tenants, while 286 men under 29 years of age took up crofting, encouraged by training and generous grants.

A crofter can no longer live on the produce of his croft. I remember as a boy early last century passing five self-supporting crofts along my two-mile walk to and from school in Tobermory. All those, and others, are all gone there, the land reverted to heather, bracken and coarse grass. I remember well the hard work with spade and perhaps a borrowed horse and cart, with several milch cows and of course poultry. Every day, on the command 'Get the cows', a collie dog set off on its own to urge the cows up the road to their pastures on the 'Big Hill', and again collected them in the evening as they leisurely grazed their way home along the grassy verges of the road. Motor cars were few and far between and the cows had the roads almost to themselves. A good dog saved the crofter much time. Then, after the harvest and through the winter, the sheaves of oats stored at the back of the byre or in the barn were threshed by flail, and the oats winnowed out in a strong wind. Life was simple and uncomplicated.

In spite of every encouragement, crofting has been slowly declining. To blame are distance from markets, penal petrol price, high freights, poor livestock prices – and the attractions of better work and prospects for young folk in the south. In fact, the cost of living in the remoter island districts can be 11% more than on the mainland. In spite of that, the Crofters Commission thinks there is about to be a revival.

The answer is diversification. Income must be augmented by part-time work such as forestry, inshore fishing, fish and shellfish farming, with improving quality of stock-raising and accommodation for summer visitors. Crofters can provide a valuable labour force for local projects. The main objective of the Commission and the chief Scottish agencies is to maintain and improve the crofting communities, which have played such an important part in preserving the unique heritage of the Highlands and Islands and the Gaelic language through the leadership of local men, whose knowledge has been handed down for generations.

The second, and perhaps the most fundamental change of all is taking place this year – 2002 – with the Land Reform (Scotland) Bill introduced by Scottish Enterprise after pressure from the Scottish Crofters' Federation to have more control over their future and the development of communities. Not only does Access to the Countryside feature in the Bill, but much more important, it almost reverses land ownership by giving crofting communities the absolute right to purchase their tenanted lands at any time, irrespective of the wishes of the landowner. This can be carried out by a simple majority vote by a community of twenty or more crofters and non-crofters, supported by the Scottish Land Court Fund.

At first this entitlement will be confined to the largest crofting area from Barra to the Butt of Lewis in the Outer Hebrides, where there are 300 communities occupying more than half the total land area. In the meantime, outwith this special area, the purchasing rights of communities can only be carried out when an estate is being sold. Behind the initial organising is the Highlands and Islands Enterprise, and the Scottish Land Court will adjudicate on disputes and matters arising, such as boundaries.

Of course there are many complications still to be

sorted out: for instance the take-over of salmon and sea trout fishings within the crofting area. Can crofters maintain them to standards acceptable by anglers? What will happen to bailiffs and others who depend on this for their livelihood? Some isolated hotels, too, are almost entirely dependent on angling rights for fishing that are the best in Europe, attracting visitors to unfrequented districts, and so helping the tourist economy. The same applies to some estates that depend on attracting wealthy tenants to help their maintenance. Then in some communities crofters are gradually becoming outnumbered by incomers who have no interest in crofting, retired people and others attracted by the environment and the quiet life. Decisions may be taken by communities by a majority vote contrary to the principles of crofting.

There can be early problems for crofters themselves when they find they have to face the financial and detailed responsibilities of being landowners. Certainly, a training scheme has been created to meet this difficulty. A community, rather than individuals, should have more collective advantages, such as bulk purchases, conveyance of livestock to markets, and official recognition and cooperation in local problems. While some crofters are eager to take up this new concession, there are some with a more cautious approach who will await the outcome of early takeovers. The legislation is aimed at bringing population and communities back into the outlying areas and by doing so broadening the scope of the whole tourist economy in the Highlands and Islands.

Part 2
The Clearances in Mull

The people are the great sanctuary of sanity, the country the last stronghold of happiness. when they disappear there is no hope for the race.

(Virginia Woolf)

1
The Structure of the Island

The island of Mull is the third largest of the Hebrides. With its mid-position and the railhead at mainland Oban just thirty miles distant, it has the advantages of easy contacts with the bustling Lowlands. It is an island of 225,000 acres in extent, measuring 24 miles from north to south and 26 from east to west, but these figures give no indication of its irregular coastline, which, with its deeply penetrating sea lochs on the west coast, measures about 300 miles. Inland the mountainous terrain means that the distance by road from Tobermory in the extreme north to Fionnphort and Iona ferry in the extreme south-west is 50 miles.

Over most of the island, the older geology is concealed by a cover of much younger rocks, especially basaltic lavas which erupted around 60 million years ago. Originally these lavas were much thicker than now and the height of Ben More, 3169 feet, was once approximately twice that. Now, at least 1km has since been eroded away from central Mull, exposing the inner workings of the old volcano and leaving Ben More close to the western edge of this centre of volcanic activity. The land surface we now see is the result of recent glaciation. The ice left the western coasts of Mull about 17 thousand years ago, but the last valley glaciers only left central Mull around 11,500 years ago. The removal of this ice load caused the Earth's crust under Mull to rebound, raising the island and leaving ancient raised beaches and uplifted sea cliffs inland from today's coastline.

The breakdown of the basaltic rocks left behind a rich volcanic soil which gathered especially on the flat areas along the shores. Less than half the island lies below the 500ft contour, where there is such rich grazing for cattle that F. Fraser Darling wrote: 'Mull is some of the most fertile land in the Kingdom, but ruined by sheep farming . . . Mull and Ulva are cattle country without equal in the Highlands. In fact, about 1800, before the invasion of sheep, Mull was exporting 2,000 head of cattle per annum, along with transit herds from the islands and nearby mainland. The grazing is so good that cattle could graze up to the 1,000ft contour in many places. In 1970 the island was still exporting 5,000 head of cattle, which unfortunately have to compete now with afforestation and sheep, which offer quicker returns to stock raisers.'

Although Mull could never compete with the extensive machair lands and crofting potential of other islands, crofting did get firmly established mainly in the flatter land of the Ross of Mull and neighbouring Iona, and the island of Ulva, and to a lesser extent on the rougher ground at Tobermory, Dervaig, Quinish, Torloisk, Salen, around the heads of Loch na Keal and between Torosay and Loch Buie, including the 'Garden of Mull'. As mentioned earlier, I remember during my schooldays at Tobermory just before World War I used to pass five or six crofts along the mile of road between our house and the school, each with a few cows that grazed in summer on the hill grazings round about, that catered for the modest requirements of the crofters. Today I believe there is not one; they were either abandoned, taken over by the few farms, or carry a stock of sheep.

2
Social History

Under the more settled conditions that followed the end of the Jacobite uprising and large families becoming common, the population of Mull rose from 5,500 in 1760 to a peak of nearly 11,000 in 1821. Many of the soldiers who returned from the Napoleonic wars found their homes and livelihood gone or under threat. The names of 116 officers alone are recorded as coming from Mull to serve in those wars, and we can only guess at the large number of men who served in the ranks who followed their remaining chiefs as of old. Later, during the Crimean war, at least one Mull laird threatened crofters with eviction unless they sent a son to serve in the army. You remember the bold old Ross-shire man who addressed the Duke of Sutherland when he was expressing his surprise that so few of his tenants were volunteering to fight: 'The men are all gone; you can send your sheep!'

From the peak in 1821 the population of Mull had fallen steeply to 5,000 as a result of evictions, migration and emigration. At the same time the population of Tobermory had risen from a much earlier figure of 200 to 850 in 1821, and 2,000 in 1871. So many crofting settlements had been cleared that homeless and jobless people crowded into the town seeking any form of work or shelter, even in outhouses and byres, reluctant to leave their island, or simply lacking enough cash to emigrate. Many had to sell their few possessions to provide food for survival, helped by the Relief Committee and the Kirk Sessions. Shellfish must have figured largely in the diet of people living near the sea. I remember when clearing a corner beside our little house in the wood above Dervaig, I came across a great dump of limpet and whelk shells which must have taken years to accumulate. Of course they may have been used to bait for line fishing, but this was a purely crofting little area a mile or more from the sea.

The more accessible industrial Lowlands were now offering work not to be found in Mull, and a drift to the south began, until 100 years later, the population of Tobermory had fallen to 600, while that of Mull remained at 2,000. There was nothing left in Mull for young folk anxious to improve their prospects. I might quote as an aside that the chief exports from the islands were doctors and ministers – Mull had its full quota of them!

As the twentieth century went on, much was done to revitalise the island of Mull. People began to return, many now finding it an ideal place for retiral. Private houses are going up, small and diversified local industries established, thanks to local initiative, progressive administration and vastly improved communications. However, the tourist trade plays a large part now in the economy, which can be precarious in an off season. Sheep and agricultural subsidies play a large part in farming returns, and nearly all crofters are dependent on part-time jobs.

3
Emigrant Ships and Their Destinations

I have traced a few details about the emigrant ships. Tobermory was a convenient centre not only for the departure of people from Mull, but from districts as far apart as Lewis and Kintyre. The voluntary emigration that had existed up to 1840 became a vital outlet for dispossessed people when the potato disease brought chaos to the whole crofting communities, and the landlords sought to get rid of those unwanted people, even by subsidising their passage fares for a few years that worked out at about £4 to £10 for an individual and £35 for a large family. Repeatedly the accusation of laziness and apathy was applied to the peasantry of the Highlands and Islands, another excuse for clearing them off the land. Their resourcefulness after emigrating into a free environment, their success as colonists, were all conveniently ignored. When settlements were being set up in the Canadian Middle West towards the end of the nineteenth century, contrary to public beliefs the name 'Calgary' was not bestowed by nostalgic emigrants from Mull. The true story is that Col. J. F. Macleod, Commander of the North-West Mounted Police (the 'Mounties') had spent some time in Calgary, in the north-west of Mull, as guest of the owner of the estate, John H. Munro Mackenzie. To perpetuate his happy memories there he asked the permission of the laird to name the new post he was setting up in Alberta as 'Calgary'. The laird was delighted to agree.

Here are a few details from the years of emigration:

1770 Some of the earliest emigrants from Mull left on the *Polly*.

1827 170 people left Tobermory on the *Stephen Wright*.

1832 1,090 emigrants from Lewis and Mull left Tobermory for Nova Scotia.

1835 More than 3,500 people from Oban, Kintyre and Mull sailed from Tobermory in four ships for Nova Scotia and Quebec.

1837 315 selected and government-assisted emigrants sailed from Tobermory on the *Brilliant* to establish official settlements abroad.

1838 *British Queen* sailed from Tobermory.

1839 *Hercules* sailed from Tobermory for Australia.

1840 550 people from Skye and Mull left for Prince Edward Island.

1846 Emergency food supply, barley, oatmeal, peas, was landed at Tobermory by the frigate *Belvidere*.

1847 Assisted passages were paid for Mull and Iona people on *Jamaica* and *Harley*.

1853 Famine victims from Ulva and elsewhere left by *British Queen*, *Panama* and *Hercules* for Australia.

1859 Emigrants to Australia and New Zealand left Tobermory by the *Marmion*, *Barlow* and *Charlotte*.

1870s Several assisted passages to Australia and New Zealand.

Special mention should be made of the *Mary Jane*, a large private yacht belonging to Sir James Matheson, proprietor of the island of Lewis, whose activities were mentioned earlier. His most beneficial act during the critical years of the 1840s was to make his yacht available free of charge to enable seasonal migrants from the Hebrides – such as at harvest time – to travel to the labour markets of the south. In 1847 alone the yacht was estimated to have carried 2,256 persons from the Hebrides to the Clyde ports.

4
The Mull Clearances, Estate by Estate

As usual, regrets come too late to be remedied. Before the '14-'18 War, when I was a boy, I listened with boredom to the stories related by visitors at our fireside. Brought up as the son of the governor of the Mull Combination Poorhouse, what a store of information I could have gathered as well from the inmates, some of whom were themselves aged victims of the Clearances. Although my father was a Mull man born and bred, and his father, my grandfather, a farm manager on the island, he was probably in his youth as little interested as I was. In his early twenties – about 1880 – he left futureless Mull and joined the Glasgow Police Force, from which he shortly volunteered for service in the Hong Kong Police Force. He retired as superintendent in 1904 and returned to Mull. I was born at my mother's home at Portmahomack in Easter Ross, just a month or two after she returned from the colony in 1903. I, too, moved from Mull to mainland bank service in the south, so both my father and I lost our contacts with Mull.

My knowledge of the Clearances comes from relatives and friends in Mull, and from some researches. It was a few years after my retiral that my wife and I returned to the little cottage in the woods near Dervaig that I

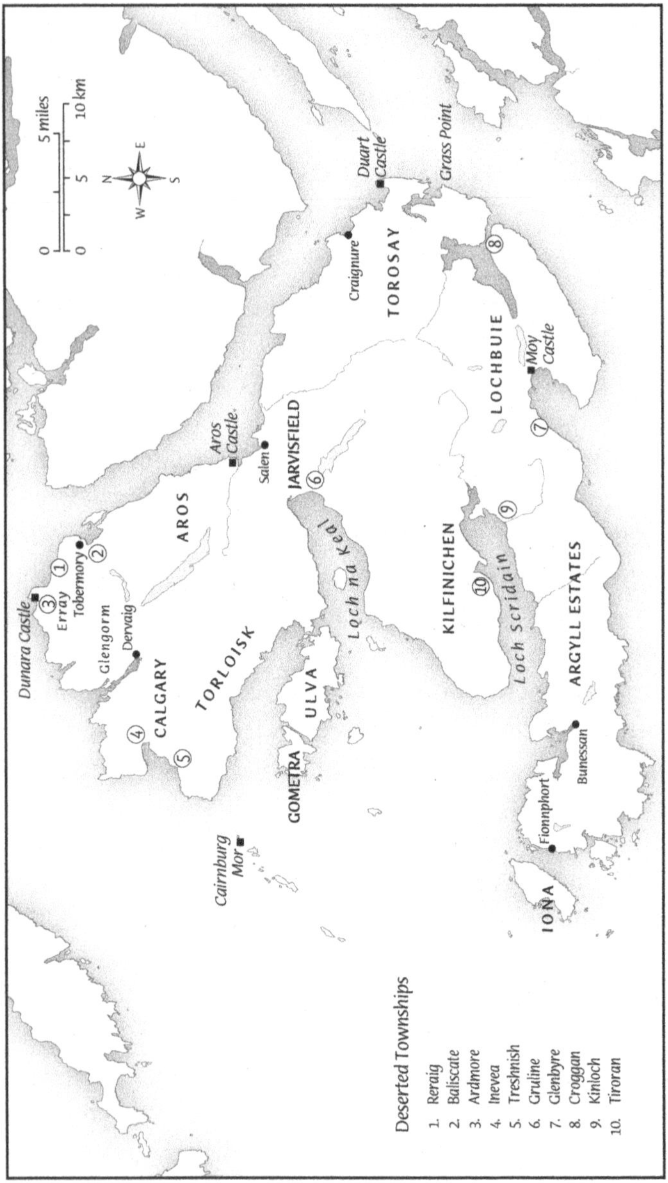
0 5 miles
0 5 10 km
N
E
S
W
Duart Castle
Grass Point
Craignure
TOROSAY
LOCHBUIE
Moy Castle
Aros Castle
Salen
JARVISFIELD
AROS
Tobermory
Dunara Castle
Erray
Glengorm
Dervaig
CALGARY
TORLOISK
ULVA
GOMETRA
Cairnburg Mor
Loch na Keal
KILFINICHEN
Loch Scridain
ARGYLL ESTATES
Bunessan
Fionnphort
IONA
Deserted Townships
1. Reraig
2. Baliscate
3. Ardmore
4. Inevea
5. Treshnish
6. Gruline
7. Glenbyre
8. Croggan
9. Kinloch
10. Tiroran

really began to learn something about the social history of the island. I have grateful memories of my long talks with my cousins Calum and Peter Maclean, Alick (Ban) MacDougall and his sister Maggie, quiet Nellie Stewart, and of course that fountain of information, Donald Mackechnie in Dervaig. To my regret, I never talked long enough with Mary Morrison, of the Penmore Mill, to tap her lifelong memories. There was Neil Patterson of Dervaig. John Sinclair, in Tobermory, who belonged to Glengorm, was a schoolmate of mine. I even remember old Donald Colquhoun there, who was a victim of the Aros estate persecution.

Then there was Chrissie MacGillivray, who latterly lived all alone at the remote sheep farm at Burg, on the National Trust property of cliffs, rocky shores, caves and the famous McCulloch's Fossil Tree I used to visit on that wild headland known as The Wilderness. Finally, I must mention that great man Seton Gordon, of Skye, who never received the public recognition he deserved for his wonderful knowledge and writings about the Highlands and Islands. With great kindness he gave me many useful snippets of little-known Mull folklore and history, with the freedom to use the information as I wished. I still have his letters, ill-typed, as he admitted, on a battered antique typewriter!

There now follows what I have been able to find about the then Mull estates and the actions of their owners during the days of the Clearances. The general locations are indicated on the accompanying sketch map. Since then most estates have been so fragmented that their boundaries today can differ considerably. I have been able to identify only one laird who showed consideration for the crofting community, apart from the earlier Ronald Maclean of Coll (who owned the north of Mull) and General MacQuarie of Jarvisfield that centred on Gruline. That was MacDonald of Gribun, who not only respected the people as 'respectable and industrious', but made available such land as he could spare for the dispossessed.

What I have written is factual, either verbatim from descendants, or extracted from the thirty books of Court that record, in 46,000 questions and answers, the evidence given before the Napier Commission of 1883 by victims of the Clearances, of undoubted integrity, from every exploited Parish in the Highlands and Islands.

Tobermory Estate*

The name 'Tobermory' is translated as 'Well of Mary' – Saint Mary. The place has an ecclesiastical connection going far back into the centuries, with the foundations of a small pre-Reformation chapel† to be seen in the old cemetery, beside which lie grave slabs of the MacKinnons of Mishnish before they relinquished the north of Mull to the Macleans. Historically, too, the bay holds all that is left of the hull of the Armada ship San Juan de Sicilia, destroyed by an internal explosion in 1588 along with the

**In fact Tobermory is not, and never was, an estate, though it formed part of Aros estate. It obtained burgh status in the nineteenth century.*

†The discovery and excavation of the eighth-century chapel at Baliscate took place after Peter had died, but he would have been delighted.

great treasure she was reputed to have carried. Later, in 1686, the Duke of Argyll, with his followers, made their first landing here in their futile support of the unhappy Duke of Monmouth. During World War II the bay was the chief centre in Britain for the training of anti-submarine forces under that formidable leader, Vice-Admiral Sir Gilbert Stephenson. I am surprised that nothing has been done in Tobermory to commemorate this war effort.* So Tobermory is a place with a long history.

In 1789 the village was selected, along with other centres, by the 'Society for Extending the Fisheries and Improvements round the United Kingdom', hereafter simply 'The Society'. The land was bought from Maclean of Coll, extending southwards towards Baliscate in the present Aros estate, with Erray to the north. High hopes for a prosperous herring industry were dashed when the shoals of unpredictable fish moved away from the area. I remember back in the 1920s seeing the rare appearance of a shoal so dense that people were scooping them on to the shore with landing nets! In any case Oban, a convenient mainland port, was only thirty miles distant along the sheltered Sound of Mull. However, Tobermory developed as a busy and convenient centre not only for Mull, but for the adjacent islands and isolated mainland, with what is probably the finest bay and anchorage in the Hebrides. A crofting community was established, and quite successful for a time.

**After this was written, a commemorative book was placed in Mull Museum for those who served in Tobermory to sign. More recently children and grandchildren of those who served became signatories, and the book has been kept in the Museum collection.*

By 1791 a Customs House and Post Office had been opened, and by 1800 there was a population of 300, with 20 stone-built houses and 30 thatched cottages. The first streets to be laid out were Argyll Terrace and Breadalbane Street, sites being allocated to the first applicants. Houses were to be built within eighteen months with a rental of one penny per foot frontage in Breadalbane Street, two-pence in Argyll Terrace with its greater amenity, all with a garden of one-sixth of an acre, with grazing rights on the hill by arrangement with the agent of the Society, and also the right to 'win' (extract) stone for building and peats as fuel. Business premises lay along the narrow waterfront, where the charge was sixpence per foot frontage and houses to be of two or more storeys. Thomas Telford was an advisor to the Society. One of his projects was the substantial inn that stood opposite the pier, now called the Old Pier. Legal titles were granted for the building lots and crofts on a 99 years' lease.

Tobermory developed rapidly, until by 1811 there were 11 registered vessels, a cooper, boatbuilder, and 28 open boats. In 1808, 136 large vessels had used the port. By 1840 there were no less than 120 crofts around the estate, and in 1845 the port of Tobermory exported 15,420 barrels of potatoes worth four shillings and sixpence (22p) per barrel. The whole of Mull was producing an estimated 30,000 barrels – and at that point the devastating potato disease swept the country and destroyed the whole crop.

The Society created over 50 individual crofts; but certain of the conditions or concessions were to lead to trouble in the future. While legal leases were held on a 99 years basis, the vital hill grazings were granted to the whole body of crofters by the verbal consent of the agent; further, those same hill grazings could be conveyed to any new owner to whom the Society's lands could be sold in the future, if the new proprietor carried out 'improvements', even fencing, and thus alienate grazing rights held by use and wont by the crofters.

By 1871 the population of Tobermory had risen to nearly 2,000. It being impossible to find any form of accommodation or work where they were living, victims of the Clearances had been coming into the town almost daily during the days of famine and persecution – even whole families packing into single rooms – in the desperate hope of finding some work there.

A typical case described by Robert Somers (quoted in The Great Highland Famine) was that of four cottars and their families who had been evicted in the Kilfinichen estate. One highly respectable family of ten was living in a single room in Tobermory, their only food thin porridge, with no furnishings other than what they had been able to save and carry across the hills for forty miles. The husband, who had been ill in Glasgow, was faced with eviction when he was able to return to his home in Kilfinichen, and the house was pulled down. All he was left with was some precarious fishing in Loch Scridain.

Many of those unfortunate people had to sell their livestock, even household possessions, at whatever price they were offered, to meet the harsh living conditions.

In 1847, 96 people evicted from neighbouring estates, and in 1850, 78 from Ulva, settled in Tobermory. These are only a few examples out of the many. This settled state of affairs – at least for the local crofters – came to an end in 1842 when the Society sold the southern, Aros, portion of the estate to David Nairne for £33,000.

Aros Estate

The first action taken by Nairne, the new owner, was to demand higher rents from the crofters who were now on his estate. Although they had long leases, they had no protection from increases in rent. The laird's lame excuse was 'The higher the rent, the better the work.' Several crofters were unable to pay the higher rent and were obliged to give up their holdings, receiving no compensation for any reclamations or improvements they had carried out during their tenancies. Nairne also suggested to the Society's factor, John McCallum, the Tobermory solicitor, that the Society should persuade the people to allow him – Nairne – to take over part of the open hill grazings that lay within his estate. As the rights to those, even verbal, were part of the 'tack' or 99-years lease, the crofters refused to consider it.

Nairne was able to carry out a few evictions where his actions could not be opposed, such as for non-payment of rents, and by high-handed actions to have several imprisoned for being too obstructive.

Between 1842 and 1845 he tried to secure a portion of the open grazing land at Baliscate by having a turf wall raised around it and claiming this as an 'improvement'. The settlers were able to bring their objection before the House of Lords, which upheld their case. Not to be outdone, Nairne applied to the Court of Session, which strangely enough decided in his favour, over-ruling the decision of the House of Lords on the technicality that a turf dyke could be accepted as 'fencing', and as such came within the definition of 'improvements' as embodied in the original settlement terms of the Society. This time the crofters were unable to meet the costs of a further appeal and were forced to submit. This was another ruse used by unscrupulous landlords, to involve tenants in expensive litigation further complicated in the Courts by the use of English in place of their universal Gaelic speech.

At Sgriobruadh several crofters were evicted on what became the local golf course early next century to make the land available for a friend of the laird. You will still see the evidence of two ruined houses, the upper, on the west side, called Achafraoch, which name was substituted later for the Mull Combination Poorhouse, which stood on the flat ground beside the river below. Overall, Nairne was able to carry out twenty evictions and the surrender of those crofts during this period.

There is a reminder of the laird's arrogance when one John MacKinnon testified before Sheriff Robertson when the Commission of Enquiry was in session later at Tobermory in 1883. MacKinnon had held at the time an unexpired period of his 99-years' lease, yet Nairne had him imprisoned for obstruction. This consisted of going into his croft and finding estate workers ploughing it up for a takeover by the laird. He ended the intrusion by halting the work and leading the horses outside his enclosure. During his absence in prison the croft was illegally taken over, ploughed, sown, and never returned, nor was any compensation paid.

In 1845 Nairne sold the Aros estate to Alexander Crawford, a much more reasonable laird. He generously offered to substitute legal titles in place of the Society's verbal permission to use the hill grazings, but strangely enough, only two of the crofters took up the offer: one Duncan, and a Captain Hugh Maclean. Could the crofters have been so browbeaten and harassed by the previous laird that they refused out of suspicion that there must be some fresh 'catch' somewhere? Apart from that, nothing controversial seems to have arisen during Crawford's ownership. He sold the estate in 1856 to Captain Farquhar Campbell, who was to take over the persecution where Nairne had left off.

He tried to clear the whole of the hill grazings, but this was bitterly opposed by the whole remaining crofters, who were described as an 'Army of Martyrs'. Although lacking legal titles, they described their entitlement as established by use and wont. The protestors were served with notices to quit, but this time they had the support of the whole community in an appeal, and Campbell lost his case, the Court holding that he had no jurisdiction. However, he interdicted the crofters in the Baliscate area, submitting this was part of his private property for which no valid title could be produced. The interdict was confined to grazing on common land and peat-cutting. A further appeal was again upheld by the House of Lords on the Society's intentions established by use and wont, with or without titles. The crofters now expected to resume their interrupted access, but were obliged to interdict the laird himself for his continuing obstructions. The proceedings were costly, but they had the continuing support of the whole community. At the proceedings one Donald Gillies had been chosen to represent the tenants, but was persuaded by Campbell's agent to withdraw. Another crofter came forward and quoted the leasing rights for such parts of the grazings as were not set aside for cultivation or improvements.

Campbell persisted by erecting a wire fence across the best part of the grazings on the north side of Lochnameall, which prevented livestock from gaining access during the heat of summer. He subsequently drained part of the loch, ostensibly trying to locate bog-iron. One could almost liken him to the traditional monster after which the loch was named. Under the 'Improvements' clause he was allowed by the myopic Court of Session to claim the newly fenced portion, whose erection had just started and was nowhere near completion when the case was still sub judice. The exasperated crofters, represented mostly by the womenfolk (rather like the militant women of Skye!), took the law into their own hands and smashed down the fence! This was described as rioting by the Law, and the ringleaders were imprisoned for ten days.

Campbell left the hill grazings in chaos and thus destroyed all the good intentions of the Society. He granted only one feu charter during his ownership. That was in 1862 for the site of a new Mull Combination Poorhouse, five acres of poor boggy land with a letting value of two shillings (l0p) per acre, or ten shillings (50p) in all. He demanded an annual feu duty of £24! By the time Alexander Allan bought the estate from Campbell, the crofters had been left with the poorest grazings, and the cutting of peat in the poorest locations. There was little left for a new owner to exploit.

Alexander Allan was quite a different type of laird. The crofting was interfered with no further, but turning his attention to the town itself he took the initiative of arranging an overdue supply of good water to the whole town, certainly at public expense, from a reservoir constructed about two miles up the Dervaig road, which became the supply point for Tobermory distillery when a new and better supply was laid on from the Mishnish Lochs, a mile further on, in the mid-twentieth century. He also arranged for a proper sewerage system to be created, whose overflow was carried some distance north of the present MacBrayne's pier. All this was rather shortsightedly complained about by the inhabitants; the costs, the inconvenience, the delays. Mr Allan also presented the Aros Hall to the town at his own expense, a much-needed amenity.

I remember hearing of two Tobermory men, one Henderson, and Donald Colquhoun, who were held to have been such critics of the laird's projects that for their temerity they were blacklisted, and their names circularised round other Mull lairds as being undesirable tenants who should be refused any favours.

Erray Estate

This estate runs north and west of Tobermory and marches with Glengorm, formerly known as Sorne and part of the nineteenth-century Quinish estate to the west and Aros to the south. Tobermory was sandwiched between.

The main object of the owner of Erray estate seems to have been to clear individual crofts and amalgamate them into compact farming units which were then let to favoured friends. The Society had so few requests from crofters for holdings on that side that in 1848 twenty vacant holdings were transferred to William Robertson, Sheriff-Substitute of North Argyll, to be added to the farming portions of the Erray estate along with the relative grazings. This was not unreasonable. However, the estate went on to evict nine people in three crofts at Reraig, and eight in two crofts at Ardmore. Four of the unallocated plots were made over to Mr Sproat, writer and bank agent at Tobermory, where a branch of the Clydesdale bank had been opened in the 1850s.

On William Robertson's death, the enlarged estate was offered to McLachlan, of Mingary, who gave it up in 1880, and the lands were let to McKell, of the Tobermory distillery, in 1883. The estate became an exclusive area. Public access was denied and the approaches to the estate closed, even the popular path along the shore to the lighthouse. Tobermory was virtually hemmed in between Aros and Erray. Even the new Burgh status and independent police control could not influence the principals to be less autocratic.

Anyone exploring the extreme north of Mull will find all the evidence he needs of the evictions in the ruined hamlets of Reraig, Ardmore, Penalbanach and Laorin, where head-high bracken now covers the once excellent crofting lands.

Quinish Estate

Quinish in the nineteenth century comprised what are now the separate estates of Glengorm and Quinish.

The centre of contention was the village of Dervaig, which lies at the head of long narrow shallow Loch Chumhainn, and is said to be one of the most picturesque villages in the Hebrides. It was built about 1800 by Hugh Maclean of Coll, whose objective was to improve the lot of the people living around Loch Chumhainn and establish a small settlement at the head of the loch in the centre of some good land. He sponsored the building of a street of two dozen stone-built houses in pairs, with large gardens at the back, crofts and more than sufficient hill grazings, all on generous terms. Today nearly all of the houses have been modernised, but there are still a few that retain the original characteristics.

Dervaig is a centre whose history goes back to prehistory with several groups of standing stones and Iron Age forts, such as one whose traces lie on the little elevation beside the bridge over the river Bellart. There is evidence of the old system of barter in later days that replaced the shortage of hard cash. If you go up Glen Bellart along the road to Salen, then in about five miles, exactly at the watershed with Glen Aros at a place they called Druim Tigh Mhic Ghillie Chatain ('Ridge of the House of the Cattanach Fellow' – the longest place name in Mull). Between the road and the edge of the modern forestry plantation you will still see traces of the old turf tables on which goods were exhibited – what you would call a 'Boot Sale' in modern times! Go back for a mile or so to where Glen Bellart flattens out, and you will see a huge isolated boulder on the west side of the burn, where it had rolled down from the escarpment above. This is called the 'Bargain Stone', where serious transactions were discussed and settled. With all this and the ruined villages, it was certainly an important centre in days gone by.

In 1847 James Forsyth became the owner of Quinish estate, that was about twenty years after Maclean of Coll had given up the north of Mull. In the same manner as the policies of the lairds of Aros destroyed the ambitions of the Society in Tobermory, so also did Forsyth destroy Hugh Maclean's development plans for Dervaig. The story of the Dervaig troubles is best told by quoting the evidence presented much later to the Napier Commission by Lachlan Kennedy, a well-respected man who acted as spokesman for his fellow crofters.

As usual, the new laird's first main target was the rents. In 1850, soon after buying the Sorne (Glengorm) estate, 27 crofters were evicted there, and in 1851 a further 52 families. Kennedy's own rent was raised without notice twice in one year. There were 27 crofters in the village with common grazings on Torr and Monabeg for 56 cows, one bull and 28 horses. Forsyth called a meeting in Dervaig and announced that in his generosity he was prepared to take over those grazings, carry out considerable improvements, and return them to the crofters in a very much more productive condition in three years. Accustomed to the former straight dealings with Hugh Maclean, the crofters trusted Forsyth's word and agreed, but nothing was committed to writing. At the end of the three years, before returning the grazings, Forsyth called another meeting, this time in his own house where his presence was so much more intimidating, and announced that in return for restoring the grazings (which he had reduced in area by ploughing certain areas and adding them to his own private land), he demanded a rent from them of £80 per annum in exchange for a 19-years' lease, with a further liability of £19 per annum for the lime and fertilisers used in making the improvements.

The incensed crofters unanimously refused to consider this imposition, whereupon the treacherous laird withdrew all future use of both the Torr and Monabeg grazings, with no corresponding reduction in rents. Further, he took over at his own valuation the livestock on both, telling the crofters they could destroy any livestock rejected by the laird that they were unable to sell. Of course the crofts rapidly deteriorated, the 27 crofts being reduced to 13, with the people struggling to make a living. Some of the crofters found it impossible to carry on, gave up and left.

Another witness, John Campbell, also testified, this time describing what happened to the tenants in the houses in the village. He described how the little community had been established, how so many of them had been allowed to build their own homes, been given a croft, a big garden, where each household could graze two cows and one horse at an annual rent of £3 14s 6d (£3.72p). Then in the spring of 1847 Forsyth demanded a meeting with the heads of families and offered new titles to their holdings if they would sign new agreements. Gaelic speakers and unfamiliar with legal documents, all but two of them signed in good faith – to discover when it was too late that they had signed away all their rights, everything except their houses and gardens, with no reduction in rents. They were obliged to exist on the produce of their gardens and nothing else.

The same witness, who had been a soldier at one time, described how he had two horses essential for ploughing. When he delayed signing, the estate workers destroyed them, with no offer of compensation.

At the other side of the estate, Glengorm, evictions had been proceeding. Here Forsyth selected an ideal site to build the fine mansion we now know as Glengorm Castle. This meant clearing three good crofts and the eviction of the tenants to provide the site for the building and its policies. The story goes that as the house was nearing completion he wished to select a suitable name for it. Dunara? he suggested; but his advisors pointed out that the ancient fort of that name lay several miles from the site. Then he condescended to consult an old woman from among the crofters still remaining. 'Call your fine house Glengorm,' she advised, with a cynicism that escaped the laird; for delighted as he was with the name, which is the Gaelic for 'Blue Glen,' he did not realise that the old woman was preserving for all time the memory of the days when the glen was indeed blue – with the smoke from the burning of homesteads. That is how the old name of Sorne became Glengorm from then on. Nearly all the district was cleared for the introduction of sheep.

Another tradition was told in the year 1917 by an old lady who had lived her whole life in Glengorm. When Forsyth was about to inspect his completed mansion and opened the front door, a bat flew out in his face. This bat, the people said, was the soul of a crofter who had been cruelly evicted, who before he died had laid a curse on the laird that he would never live to sleep in the house. Strangely enough, Forsyth took ill and died before he could take up residence.

I like a refreshing story about the woman who successfully defied the laird that was told to me by the late John Sinclair, Tobermory, who had been brought up in Glengorm. This was about an elderly widow who infuriated Forsyth by his inability to force her to give up her croft beside the shore. She and her husband had been given the title of this holding in perpetuity by Maclean of Coll in recognition of their long faithful service, when he was severing his connection with North Mull. Not even the laird could dispute this title. He tried to discourage her by every minor persecution, such as interdicting her from crossing his land, leaving her cut off except by sea. Yet somehow she was never short of supplies and help around the croft. The few neighbours who could visit her were mystified, but she explained that she was helped by the Little People (the elves and good fairies) who came in the night. She always left a plate of porridge and milk for them at the back door as a thank you. When the neighbours tried this, the plate was certainly empty next morning, but there was no trace of the Little People!

The secret was this: her son, who owned a smack and carried goods between the islands, used to slip in to the shore near the cottage on favourable nights and attend to her needs. Further, in retaliation for the laird's persecutions of his mother, strange incidents began to occur around the estate; axle pins disappeared from carts, whose wheels fell off under a heavy load; 100 prize sheep fell over a cliff to their death; the stackyard, with the supply of hay for the livestock, went up in flames! The young man and his one or two deckhands were never caught, for they were guided or warned by signals from a lighted candle at the window of the tiny attic of the laird's house occupied by the servant girl whom the son subsequently married!

Mornish Estate, Better Known as Calgary

This was one of the fragmented districts in Mull sold by the Argyll Estates for the Duke of Argyll. It was bought by Capt. Allan McAskill in 1823, when he built Calgary

House, or Castle as it is sometimes known, in its sheltered woods overlooking the sands and machair of lovely Calgary Bay. At once he completely cleared the townships of Arin and Inevea that overlooked the steep opposite side of the Bay. Inivea in particular is an excellent example of the building designs of its day, with the ruins still standing up to the 'wa-heids', as they are called in the south, the flat tops of the walls on which the rafters were laid. Other clearances were carried out at Caliach and Treshnish, and Calgary Bay was a calling place for some emigrant ships.

Torloisk Estate

This was owned by the Marquis of Northampton, who was connected by marriage with the old family of the Macleans of Torloisk, one of whose early chiefs was Ailean na Sop, a reformed pirate. The estate lies along the north side of Loch Tuath with some of the finest views in Mull across the island of Ulva and the sea lochs to Ben More and the central mountains. Thirty-two evictions were carried out by the factor in order to extend the private lands of the proprietor. Neil Patterson, of Dervaig, was born at Crackaig in 1860, half a mile from a similar settlement, Glacgugairidh (Hollow of the Dark Grazings) which stands in a sheltered hollow at the edge of the 100ft cliff that runs along above the shore for miles. Just below the settlement there is a cave under the cliff in which are the foundations of what must have been a miniature distillery in the days of illicit distilling, well camouflaged from sea or shore. Neil described how he and other youngsters from scattered townships attended Reudle School, now a gaunt isolated ruin standing above the main road at the foot of the steep Ensay hill.* Each pupil was expected to take a peat with him daily for the fire in the schoolroom, on which you can still see old graffiti, ships in full sail, names such as Robert MacDougall, 1894 – most likely one of the MacDougall family of Haunn township, hardy inshore fishermen. Calum Alister MacDougall, who lived to be 100, was an uncle of mine by marriage. In fact, two brothers married my two aunts, and their progeny, Alick (Ban), Peter and Calum were cousins of mine. Distance was of no consequence to the pupils of those days, who travelled miles to and from school by tracks across the hills.

Two ladies of undoubted veracity told me that during a visit to Glacgugairidh they distinctly saw a figure moving into one of the houses, but when they cautiously looked in there was no sign of anyone. There was a communal garden in which I saw the old ash tree where, according to the story, a woman hanged herself from a branch. Truly an eerie place after dusk!

Ulva, and Its Smaller Neighbour Gometra

Perhaps the most heartless and extensive clearances in Mull occurred here, carried out by a laird who must have

**The school is no longer a gaunt ruin and has been renovated as a private house. A wall of graffiti from the school has been preserved, with the initials of some pupils and drawings of ships in full sail. Photographs of this can be seen in Mull Museum.*

had a sadistic obsession. Ulva, five miles from east to west and two from north to south, is an island with a long and fascinating history. For nearly 800 years it was the land of the Clan MacQuarrie whose chiefs lived in the old dun-fort of Glacingaline beside the narrow strait dividing Ulva from Gometra. In the eighteenth century the chief moved to a more conventional residence near the present Ulva House. A wall in the present factor's house is part of the original building. This is where the MacQuarrie chief entertained Dr Johnson and Boswell in 1773.

At Ferinanardy there are the ruins of the cottage where Neil (Mor) Livingstone, grandfather of the famous Dr David Livingstone, lived as a crofter until 1792, when the family moved to the south and settled at Blantyre. Neil (Bheag), the father of Dr Livingstone, was born in Ulva in 1788, the Doctor himself at Blantyre in 1813.

Neil (Mor) and his two brothers, who lived at Ballachulish, defied the authorities in 1756 by secretly taking down and reverently interring the bones of James Stewart, James of the Glen, and throwing into the sea the hated gibbet on which he had hung in chains under military guard for four years after the most infamous trial in Scottish history in 1752. James Stewart was completely innocent of the murder of Colin Campbell, known later as the Red Fox; yet at a rigged trial at Inveraray, before a Campbell jury and a Campbell judge (the Duke of Argyll himself), the outcome was an expression of the hatred the Campbells had for the Stewarts. The three brothers left the district at once and Neil finally settled safely in Ulva.

Another famous personality connected with Ulva was Lt. General Lachlan Macquarie, who is still remembered in Australia as the 'Father of Australia'. His father was a farmer in Ulva. He was Governor-General of New South Wales from 1810 to 1821, after which he retired to live in his Mull estate of Jarvisfield looking over to Ulva. He explored and opened up the colony, and he and his wife so revolutionised the lives of the convicts sent to Botany Bay that it is recorded that the harshness of life and justice in Britain encouraged such crimes as stealing a sheep to ensure deportation to the happier environment of Botany Bay.

More romantically, Thomas Campbell, who was to become Poet Laureate, wrote – among other local poems – 'Lord Ullin's Daughter', well known in our schooldays, which describes the fate of the 'Chief of Ulva's Isle' along with the daughter of Sir Allan Maclean, when eloping across the ferry to Ulva in a storm closely pursued by her father and his men. It must have been the longer crossing from Gribun to Ulva rather than the short crossing from the Torloisk side we know today. When he wrote the poem Thomas Campbell was a tutor at Sunipol House in the north of Mull.

The social history was to become grim. Unsettled days followed after 1804 when the 16th MacQuarrie chief was obliged to sell the island to pay off his indebtedness, leaving a contented, self-supporting people to their fate. The island was sold to three successive purchasers. One of them was the rather flamboyant Ronald MacDonald of Staffa, who went bankrupt in 1817. Finally, Ulva was bought in 1835 by a wealthy incomer, Francis W. Clark, who had been Sheriff of Stirling in the 1820s and '30s.

In 1837 the island had a population of 604, which increased to 851 by 1841; admittedly a high number, but the island was outstandingly fertile and allowed them to sustain their traditional way of life. In fact, it was Clark himself who supplied the statistics of the island for the *Statistical Account* of the island published in 1845. He described it as an island of outstanding fertility, his successful experiments in growing new crops such as wheat and peas, and the export of about 900 barrels of high-quality potatoes from his own home farm. He praised even the quality of the kelp produced from the shores, for there was a short resumption of the industry in the 1840s. The evidence of witnesses who appeared years later before the Napier Commission in 1883 revealed what followed in Ulva. I shall mention two of them – Lachlan MacQuarrie and A. M. Fletcher.

As a measure of the Clark's clearances that began to take effect in 1850, only 51 people were left by 1881, crowded into a corner of the island near the present ferry known as Desolation Point. Even that number was regarded as temporary, for they were forbidden to build houses or plant trees, in case this indicated some degree of permanence. The island is still dotted with the ruins of townships and cot-houses burned down by the factor and estate workers on Clark's orders. The laird's first step was to evict 73 households after moving them to smaller unproductive holdings, leaving a total of 350 people destitute. They were cottars, who as I have explained occupied their land as in days gone by under the chief, as their forefathers had done, with no legal titles. Any family trying to protest or appeal simply had the roof torn off and the house burned down, often without giving time for the occupants to remove their possessions. One old woman who was described as bedridden and cared for by her daughter was left with only a corner of the roof to keep the rain off her bed.

I have already described my background as a boy before World War I in Mull Combination Poorhouse, where my father was in charge of many old lonely inmates crippled with their lives' hardships. I have two unforgettable memories. An old man once said to me: 'When I was a boy like you, I remember my father carrying me out of the little cottage my grandfather had built. We were hardly out of the door than the factor and his men waiting outside put their blazing torches in the thatch and told us to clear out. We lost everything.'

The other memory is of an old woman who said to me: 'When I was left a young widow, of course I had to give up our home and croft. I went to see Mr. Clark and asked him if he could give me some wee place for shelter. He said "Why should I? I am not your father; but I'll tell you what I'll do for you. I am on the committee of the new poorhouse at Tobermory and I shall see to it that you are admitted."' This must have been after 1862 when the new establishment was built.

Some of the laird's actions reported by witnesses were incredible. With his own hands he tore washing from the lines and filled in a well with stones as a punishment for people temporarily obliged to live within sight of his windows. Again, he tried to ingratiate himself with the children by handing out biscuits in the hope that this would persuade their parents to cooperate with the kind laird! Everything hastened to an end following the effects of the dreaded potato disease, and Ulva suffered such evictions and persecutions that finally nothing was left but a large sheep farm and a handful of estate workers.

The foregoing are only a few of the authentic incidents reported in the evidence of reputable witnesses before the 1883 Commission.

The dislike in which Clark was held comes down in the tradition that when he died, his empty coffin, when delivered at the ferry slipway, could not be moved until an appropriate spell had been invoked to release it from the powers of evil. He must rest uneasily within the little walled burying place on the top of that little steep hillock beside the eastern shore.

How heartening it is today that the island is being revitalised.* Visitors are welcomed in increasing numbers every year. Paths are being restored, information provided, the small Telford-designed church is to be admired, and easy access is being made along the south-east shore to explore the amazing extent of worn-down, basaltic columns, so like the stonework of ancient buildings that the place became known as 'The Castles'. The estate runs a herd of pedigree cattle well-known at the markets and shows of the mainland: but always an echo of the sad old days seems to remain.

***This revitalisation continued with the community buyout of Ulva in 2018, though Jamie Howard as landowner did much before that.**

Jarvisfield Estate

This was the present Gruline estate, extended and renamed after being bought by Lt. General Lachlan Macquarie. Lt. General Macquarie bought about 10,000 acres of this land from Murdoch Maclaine of Lochbuie at a price of £1 per acre. In 1804 he renamed the estate Jarvisfield, in memory of his first wife who had died ten years earlier, Further purchases of land were made from the Argyll Estates, until, at his death in 1824, the estate covered 21,000 acres. It extended from Glen Forsa on the Sound of Mull to the village of Salen, and across the isthmus to Gruline, on Loch na Keal, where he could look across to Ulva, where his father had farmed. It included some of the most spectacular scenery in central Mull. He and his family lie in that little mausoleum that stands beside the access road to Gruline House. For a long time this little plot and the museum were maintained by the Government of New South Wales.

In 1808 he established the village of Salen as a road centre, with sixteen crofts, an inn, a shop, and resident tradesmen. He contributed to the building costs of substantial stone-built houses. A pier was built, but its location had to be moved on two later occasions to cater for the increasing size of ships and an adverse tidal flow. Later in the nineteenth century Salen was to find itself surrounded to within half a mile by sheep farms and sporting estates. The General was never responsible for any clearances; on the contrary, his ambitions for the people resembled those of Maclean of Coll at Dervaig.

Torosay Estate

This is the nearest corner of Mull to the mainland at Oban, just nine miles distant from Grass Point, where there is a small harbour and pier which used to be the focal point of all the drove roads in Mull for transport to the mainland. Torosay was another part of the Argyll Estates sold by the Duke of Argyll to Campbell of Possil in 1820. The new owner proceeded to clear the estate of unwanted tenants, but the only recorded details refer to the clearing of 34 holdings, 170 people, from a few small townships in Glen Forsa to make way for large farms. Artefacts found in the glen, especially round Callachally, prove that it was populated back to the Iron Age, or even earlier. The glen extends from the Sound of Mull to meet Glen More under that shapely hill, Ben Talaidh, the 'Prospect Hill'. The village of Salen, and the modern car ferry terminus at Craignure, lie within the estate.

In 1875 the estate was bought by Murray Guthrie, and in 1911 he sold Duart Castle and 400 adjoining acres to Sir Fitzroy Maclean, 10th Baronet of Duart and chief of the Clan Maclean, which had dominated the Isle of Mull until driven out by the Campbells in 1692. The ancestral centre of the Clan Maclean was now restored after a gap of 200 years, and the ruined castle was rebuilt and re-occupied in 1912 by Sir Fitzroy.

What we know today as the 'Salen Show', held by the Mull and Morvern Agricultural Society every August in the 'Field of the Englishman' – one of the many

Mull stories – near Aros Bridge, originated well over 200 years ago as a horse-fair held every 21st August within the Parish of Torosay. There were extensive woodlands in Torosay up to the late eighteenth century, but they were cut down to provide charcoal for the Lorne Furnace Company of Argyll, and possibly at Bonawe as well, to provide charcoal for gunpowder and explosives for the Navy and for the developing industries in the south.

The only public railway in the Scottish islands ran from the Craignure ferry terminus for over a mile to picturesque Torosay Castle with its famous walks, garden and well-wooded policies. The railway ran on a gauge of 10½ inches.

Lochbuie, with Glenbyre and Croggan

Lochbuie estate, the former lands of the Maclaines of Lochbuie, lies south and west of Torosay along part of the rugged cliff-lined coast of Mull, extending to Loch Scridain towards the west.

It may be that the wholesale clearances carried out here, which were replaced by a more profitable source of revenue, were prompted desperately even then by a mounting indebtedness. By the twentieth century the estate was heavily mortgaged, and ownership by the chief was lost through a delay of only a few hours in the repayment of an instalment, which was seized upon by the mortgagee as an excuse to foreclose. Perhaps the actions of some of the other Mull lairds were copied by Lochbuie, finding that the revenue from a sporting estate, especially deer stalking, became a more profitable and economical source of income than gathering rents from a peasantry. On the way to old Moy Castle and the mansion house that replaced it as a residence, you will see a handsome pyramidal cairn erected, as the plaque says '. . . by Lochbuie and his Highlanders . . .' in 1902, to mark the coronation of King Edward VII. Perhaps the inscription should have read '. . . and his surviving Highlanders . . .', for long before that the estate had been swept clear of his people and turned into a sporting estate.

In 1894 the newspaper *Oban Times* reported as follows:

'In 1884 there were 91 households with 500 people engaged in crofting and fishing, a comparatively prosperous community: by 1894 there remained 42 households and 250 people. Crofts had been taken over by Maclaine of Lochbuie and amalgamated into a deer forest. The countryside is dotted with ruins.'

In the area of Kinloch and Loch Buie there were 10,000 acres, including some of the finest grazings and arable land in Mull as a result of the geological limestone formations. Most of it became a sporting estate, with three shooting lodges and only a handful of gamekeepers and staff. There was one shocking action of which some lairds were guilty, and Lochbuie was one of them. In the days of near famine, the government could hardly avoid augmenting the supplies of oatmeal and other food distributed to the hardest hit and landless people. Unwisely, distribution was placed in the hands of lairds, and it emerged in evidence that not only had some of them diverted the rations to subsidise workers on their own private estates, but were even feeding them to the horses! Shooting lodges and roads in the Lochbuie estate were reported to have been built in return for food.

Two witnesses before the Napier Commission gave evidence that in 1861 there were 25 people in the township of Kinloch, at the head of Loch Scridain. They were evicted in 1865, and their 15 crofts, along with the hill grazings, combined to form two farms. This was carried out even after the rents had been increased substantially. Those callous evictions certainly led to the deaths of several old people who were forced to live under new and indescribable conditions without care or comforts.

Kilfinichen Estate

In 1849, on the Argyll Estates at Kilfinichen, which lies on the north side of Loch Scridain and extends west to Tiroran and Burg, the 8th Duke summarily evicted 32 families and took over their holdings. 25 people emigrated to America at their own expense after being threatened with further action if they failed to cooperate. Others moved to the notorious southern area at Kinloch, where they lived in poverty, forbidden to cultivate field or garden, yet having to meet inflated rents of £5 to £15 per annum. In despair, the people sold what was left of their livestock and even their household belongings, and ended up destitute.

Memories of this, handed down by her grandmother, were related by Chrissie MacGillivray, who lived latterly on her own at Burg sheep farmhouse, now owned, with the headland of Burg, by the National Trust for Scotland, at the end of a five-mile rough track from Tiroran. I often called there when on my way to explore the cliffs and amazing McCulloch's Fossil Tree in the cliffs.

Her grandmother referred to some of the incidents. Before their houses were demolished there was one blind, bedridden old woman who went to live with her niece at Tiroran. The family contracted measles, and the old woman had to be moved into the byre, with the rain pouring from the roof.

In 1847, when Poor Relief was distributing rations after the potato famine, an old woman was living in a tiny windowless room. She had her five pounds (weight) of rationed oatmeal stopped because she had an able-bodied son who was expected to support her, even although he lived with his family a long way off and probably needed assistance himself.

It was Chrissie's grandmother, Mary MacDonald, who spoke nothing but the Gaelic, who composed that lovely hymn – Leanabh an Aigh, Child in the Manger – all fourteen verses in the Gaelic, that was set to music in the 1920s.

The area around Kinloch was bought by a Mr Mitchell in 1873. On the south side of Loch Scridain there was wholesale misery. The north side was much more fertile and attractive and with a large peasantry, but this was systematically cleared by Mitchell. He suggested rather vaguely to the dispossessed people that they could change over to fishing for a living; but they were pastoral by nature and inheritance and had neither boats, gear, or expertise. Unlike the Duke of Argyll, Mitchell made neither money nor loans available to encourage them.

The Argyll Estates

Finally, I am describing what happened in the Ross of Mull and Iona. The fertile soil here makes the promontory the main crofting district in Mull. Geologically, it differs from the basaltic soils of the rest of Mull, being an area of red or pink granite which breaks down into a soil of a different composition. The granite from the Tormore quarry just north of Fionnphort (Iona Ferry) was quarried until the early twentieth century and exported by sea from a pier in the 'Bullhole' below, connected by a tramway, for ornamental and building projects at home and overseas. The structure of Iona is different again, being formed by some of the oldest rock in the world that again breaks down into good soil. It is strange how long ago the people seemed to have an instinctive awareness of the permanence of Iona, that induced kings and dignitaries to seek burial there, apart from the sanctity of the island. An old Gaelic saying describes how Iona will still be standing when 'Mull and Islay are below the sea'.

This was part of the lands of the Macleans of Duart taken over by the Campbells in 1692. By the end of the nineteenth century the Dukes of Argyll had sold portions of Mull until their only possession was here in the Ross of Mull.

Unlike so many of the new landlords, the Dukes of Argyll had at first as a general theory of amalgamating scattered uneconomic holdings into large farm units, which would both improve the living standards of the people and yield higher rents. This could only be done by getting rid of a large surplus population which was achieved by methods common to the Clearances areas of the Highlands and Islands.

As early as 1774 the 5th Duke of Argyll introduced the benefits of smallpox vaccinations. Early in the nineteenth century Argyll Estates tried to interest the crofters in a variety of jobs such as flax growing, weaving and fishing. In fact, loans were granted for the purchase of boats and gear, and even experienced advisors were brought in; but this was by tradition a pastoral people and it was difficult to change their way of life, so the good intentions of the Dukes met with little success.

Some relief was even provided for large families hard-hit by storm damage. There was a short-lived revival of the kelp industry which was of mutual benefit. This fertile land had a surplus of barley and potatoes, rather like Ulva before it was cleared, the people were self-sufficient, the population increasing. After 1800 the old run-rig system of cultivation was being steadily replaced by individual crofting, but with no security of tenure beyond a year. In fact, in their earlier consideration for the people, the Dukes remind me strongly of the well-known words from the poem by Lewis Carroll:

> 'I weep for you' the Walrus said:
> 'I deeply sympathize.'

> With sobs and tears he sorted out
> Those of the largest size . . .

There was this large majority of cottars, whom the unpopular factor John Campbell was to describe as 'locusts on the land'. While it is thought that the Dukes were not always aware of the harsh acts of their factors, they must accept the responsibility.

Land was being steadily taken over for sheep. In fact, as early as 1805 the 5th Duke boasted that his Mull and Morvern lands had more sheep to the acre than perhaps anywhere in all Britain! However, it was not until between 1840 and 1860 that some tolerance gave way to blatant greed when the 8th Duke took over, and his actions began to conform to the general pattern. Evictions became a standard policy. Rent in arrears, non-renewing of tenancies, any excuse served; yet rents were increased by up to 100%, even although the finances of the Argyll Estates showed a steady annual surplus. On only two years was there a deficit, in 1847 and 1849, but this was when the Duke was subsidising emigration, with an offer of £10 per family, thus releasing even more land by reducing the population. The lifestyle of the Dukes of Argyll both socially and politically were understandably a financial burden, but the actions in sustaining this by such methods amounted to nothing but selfish greed.

There was widespread destitution, and many people reduced to pauperism. The hard-pressed Parish Councils, assisted by the Relief Commission, brought in meal to avert starvation. In this action the Duke refused to cooperate, although he did arrange for the transport of a shipload of supplies from the Clyde. At first the landowners were unwisely appointed to distribute the supplies, but many of them demanded in payment work within their own estates instead for the benefit of the community. The Duke's factor took full advantage of this. Rents still went up and up, beyond the abilities of most of the landholders to pay, thus forcing them to give up their homes.

Between 1847 and 1860, with assisted emigration, nearly 1,100 people left the Parish. Over the same period the total population of Mull dropped by 28%, although that of Tobermory had risen as we explained earlier. All the foregoing is based on evidence given before the Commission.

In Iona, exactly the same conditions applied, and it would be wearisome to go into further details, except that statistics speak for themselves. Between 1780 and 1835 the population increased from 200 to 500. By 1881 only 250 remained.

A new age began for the few remaining hard-pressed tenants when the Napier Commission took over.

References

Proceedings of the Royal Commission (Highlands and Islands), 1892.

Statistical Accounts, 1792, 1795, 1845.

Alexander Mackenzie, *History of the Highland Clearances*, Alex Maclaren & Sons, Glasgow, 1883.

Eric Richards, *History of the Clearances*, Volume 2, Croom Helm, 1985.

T. M. Devine, *The Great Highland Famine*, John Donald, Edinburgh, 1981.

Austin Bourke, *The Visitation of God? The Potato and the Great Irish Famine*, edited by Jacqueline Hill and Cormac O'Grada, Lilliput Press, 1983.

Alain Collier, *The Crofting Problem*, Cambridge University Press, 1953.

Crofters Commission, *The Way Forward* (Highland Renewal), Inverness.

F. Fraser Darling, *West Highland Survey*, Oxford University Press, 1955.

E. Mairi MacArthur, *Iona: Living Memory of a Crofting Community, 1750–1914*, Edinburgh University Press, 1990.

Alan MacQuarrie, *Iona through the Ages*, Society of West Highland and Island Historical Research, 1983.

P. A. Macnab, *Mull and Iona*, David & Charles, 1970.

Carol Riddell, *Tireragan: A Township on the Ross of Mull: A Study in Local History*. This describes the present restoration of Tireragan, the remains of an old township in the Ross of Mull. Published by Highland Renewal at Knockvologon, Fionnphort, Isle of Mull, PA66 6BN, 1996.